The Goat in the Chile Patch

Folklore

Lada Josefa Kratky

English version by
Sheron Long

Illustrated by
Frank Remkiewicz

■■■® HAMPTON-BROWN BOOKS
Creative Materials for Active Learning™

Hampton-Brown Books
P. O. Box 223220
Carmel, California 93922

Printed in the United States of America

ISBN 1-56334-184-0

98 99 10 9

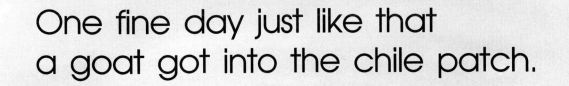

One fine day just like that
a goat got into the chile patch.

Rigo ran at the goat,
"Get out! Go away!
You'll chew no more chiles
of mine today."

But, oh! UH-OH!
The goat was not the one to go.

Then along came the rooster.

"Listen, my friend, just let me crow
and that old goat will go, you know."

So the rooster crowed
at the goat,
"Cock-a-doodle-doo!
That's enough of you!"

But, oh! UH-OH!
The goat was not the one to go.

Then along came the dog.

"Listen, my friend, just let me growl
and that old goat will go, and how!"

So the dog growled
at the goat,
"Grr-grr-grr, bow-wow!
Get out, goat. Get out now!"

But, oh! UH-OH!
The goat was not the one to go.

Then along came the pony.

"Listen, my friend, just let me neigh and that old goat will go away."

So the pony neighed
at the goat, "I-i-ay! I-i-ay!
Hey, old goat,
get out of my way!"

But, oh! UH-OH!
The goat was not the one to go.

Then along came the bull.

"Listen, my friend, just let me moo
and that old goat will know
what to do."

So the bull mooed at the goat,
"Moo, moo, mooooooo!
Hey, old goat, you're
all through!"

But, oh! UH-OH!
The goat was not the one to go.

13

Then along came the ant.

"Listen, my friend, I'm little, I know.
But I can make that old goat go."

And that's exactly what the little
ant did.

She climbed up
the goat's leg.

She crawled
across his back.

She inched her way
into his ear,
and there she bit
him hard—oh, dear!

15

And that old goat ran off
like the wind.
Where did he go?
No one knows, but he never
bothered Rigo again.